Introduction

Caribbean cuisine is a delicious melting pot, drawing ingredients and cooking methods from Europe, Africa, Asia, and the Americas, and combining them with the native foods of the islands. Caribbean cooks have absorbed these influences in a unique way, creating their own culinary art over the centuries. Although each island has its specialties, many dishes are island wide and will often have different names on different islands. Recipes may also vary from island to island, as they do from kitchen to kitchen, but the common denominator in Caribbean cooking is the use of fresh herbs and spices. Seasonings are essential to the sunny cuisine of the Caribbean, and the liberal (yet judicious) use of seasonings can often make the difference between a good dish and a scrumptious dish.

Similarly, hot peppers (chillies/capsicums), are frequently used for flavour and/or heat but, when used too generously, can be disastrously fiery. Peppers come in many varieties, but a good guide is the redder they are, the hotter they are. Peppers are used whole for stews, fricasses, etc., but can also be used chopped with the seeds removed. Please use gloves or a knife and fork when preparing them. Also, be sure to protect your eyes.

The following concoction is considered a basic seasoning:

1 medium onion, chopped	sprig each of parsley,
1 clove garlic, minced	thyme and marjoram
3 blades shallots/chives,	1/4 tsp allspice
including some green	1/2 tsp salt
tops	freshly ground black
small piece hot pepper,	pepper
deseeded, chopped	dash of Worcestershire
	sauce

Chop ingredients very fine and mix together. The mixture will keep, in a sealed container in the refrigerator, for weeks. The seasoning is used to rub into fish, poultry and meat. Incisions may be made in the food and seasoning inserted, to enable the flavours to penetrate deeper.

An old-time method of adding flavour to food in the Caribbean is that of using either burnt sugar (caramel), or rubbing sugar directly onto it before the browning process begins. Browning, for gravy, is now available commercially, so most cooks do not go to the trouble of making their own.

For many, the tantalising aroma produced by this technique brings back childhood memories of when all the mouth-watering dishes were prepared in a buck pot, known by some as a black pot, on a wood and coal stove or coal pot – before the days of electricity or gas of course!

Originally the word Creole referred to people born in the West Indies, of European descent. Today, however, it is more often applied to the cuisine of the region and

Caribbean Creole cookery is steadily making its mark wherever cooking is an important feature of daily living.

Sop Biscuits

This is a good 'filler-upper' at breakfast time for those ravenous appetites so often found in youngsters – especially at the seaside where they may have been up since dawn playing beach cricket, surfing or collecting shells along high water mark.

For this quick and simple meal, hard boil an egg, discard the shell, then slice it neatly and put to one side. Place six large plain biscuits around the bottom and sides of a colander. Slowly pour boiling water (you will need a kettleful) over them until softened and transfer biscuits to a heated plate. Spread with butter, sprinkle with salt and pepper to taste and decorate with the egg slices.

The biscuits cool very quickly so you must work fast to get them to table while still hot.

Johnny Bakes

Perhaps these may best be described as similar to a scone – a creole scone. They are popular throughout the Caribbean islands and are baked or fried. 'Bakes' are served at any meal and, as the alternate name, Journey Cakes, indicates, are popular for picnics or on jobs where a snack meal is necessary.

8 oz/225 g/2 cups flour	2 tsp baking powder
2 tbsp lard or butter	2 tsp sugar
½ tsp salt	¼ pt/150 ml/⅔ cup milk

Sift dry ingredients into bowl, then rub in the fat until mixture resembles breadcrumbs. Pour the milk in and stir to make a soft dough. Knead on a floured board then refrigerate for 30 minutes. Break dough into lemon-sized pieces, roll into balls and flatten to ½ in/1 cm thickness. Fry these in hot oil until golden or bake in a hot oven, gas mark 7, 425°F, 220°C. While still hot tear bakes open and butter generously.

Coconut Crisps

These snacks are very popular and often served with drinks prior to lunch or dinner. It is important to purchase your mature, brown coconut carefully. Choose one that is dark in colour and shake it to ensure it contains liquid. Check the 'eyes' at the top; they should be dry and not mouldy.

Now, pierce the 'eyes' of the coconut with an ice pick or skewer, drain the liquid and reserve it for another use. Bake the coconut in a preheated oven at gas mark 6, 400°F, 200°C for 15 minutes then break it with a hammer and remove the flesh from the shell, levering it out carefully with the point of a strong knife.

Peel off the brown membrane and slice the flesh into thin pieces with a potato peeler. Place these on a baking sheet, in a single layer, sprinkle with salt and bake for 20 minutes in a preheated oven at gas mark 4, 350°F, 180°C.

You may also lightly fry them in deep fat, drain and then sprinkle with salt.

Brule Johl

This dish is thought to have originated in Trinidad. There are several variations to the spelling but I believe mine to be the colloquial patois pronunciation of 'brule gueule', meaning burnt mouth/throat. Brule johl is best known as an hors d'oeuvre and served with plain biscuits but is also delicious served in half an avocado from which the seed has been removed but the skin left on.

---

1 lb/450 g good quality salt fish, soaked in water overnight
2 medium onions, finely chopped
about 2 tbsp olive oil
squeeze of fresh lime juice
2 small sweet peppers, green and red, diced
2 tsp hot sauce or 1 small hot pepper, deseeded and chopped

Flake the fish into a bowl, removing bones, skin and dark flesh. Mix in the onion, olive oil, lime juice, sweet peppers and hot sauce. Stir well and taste for adjustment in seasonings. Cover tightly and refrigerate, stirring occasionally so that the flavours blend. This will last for several days.

Breadfruit Vichyssoise

Captain Bligh brought the original breadfruit plants to the Caribbean at the end of the eighteenth century. Since then they have become an important staple food.

Despite its name breadfruit is not used as a fruit, but is in fact a very versatile, starchy vegetable. White or sweet potatoes may be substituted.

2 tbsp butter or margarine	1 ¾ pt/ 1 l./ 4 cups chicken stock
3 medium onions, finely chopped	salt and freshly ground black pepper to taste
1 clove garlic, finely minced	½ pt/ 300 ml/ 1 cup light cream or yogurt
8 oz/ 225 g breadfruit, peeled, decored and diced (or canned)	1 heaping tbsp shallots/ chives, chopped
¼ tsp hot pepper, deseeded and chopped (optional)	

Melt the butter in a heavy-bottomed saucepan and sauté onions and garlic until transparent. Add remaining ingredients, except cream and shallots. Cover and simmer until the breadfruit is tender. Cool, put into a blender, add the cream and process until smooth, adjusting the seasonings if necessary. Refrigerate until thoroughly chilled. Serve in chilled bowls and decorate with the shallots.

Callaloo Soup

This is probably the best known of all soups in the Caribbean. The main ingredients are taro leaves – often called dasheen – and okras, both originally brought to the region from Africa in the seventeenth century.

1 lb/450 g callaloo leaves, or spinach as substitute	4 shallots/chives, using green and white parts, chopped
3 pt/1¾ 1./7 cups chicken stock	¼ tsp thyme
1 large onion, finely chopped	1 whole chilli (optional)
8 oz/225 g salt beef, chopped	12 young okras or 10 oz package
freshly ground black pepper	8 oz/225 g crab meat

Remove thick stems of leaves, chop roughly and put into saucepan with all the ingredients except okras and crab. Cover and simmer until meat is tender. Add the okras, cook for 8 minutes, remove pepper and blend. Add crab, reheat and adjust seasonings. Serve piping hot with slices of avocado pear and hot bread.

Pumpkin and Split Pea Soup

The ingredients for this popular and nourishing soup are available all year round. It may also may be made in advance and stored in the deep freeze.

---

1 lb/450 g/2 cups yellow split peas	1 lb/450 g salt beef, fat removed, diced
4 large onions, sliced	piece of fresh chilli, chopped
4 tbsp butter or margarine	few dashes of aromatic bitters
3 pt/1¾ 1./7 cups chicken stock	freshly ground nutmeg
1 lb/450 g pumpkin, peeled and diced	

Rinse and pick over the peas and soak overnight in clear water. Sauté the onions in butter in a large, heavy-bottomed saucepan then add the remaining ingredients. Cover and simmer for about 1½ hours or until peas soften. Allow the soup to cool and then purée in a blender. Adjust the seasoning and reheat before serving with a little nutmeg sprinkled on top.

Spinners/Dumplings

With soup these are all-time favourites for young and old alike – in homes both humble and grand. Recipes are myriad, resulting in light, heavy, sweet and not-so-sweet etc, concoctions. They are sometimes made with corn meal in addition to flour.

2 oz/50 g/¼ cup margarine	3 oz/75 g/¾ cup flour
	salt and pepper
1 egg yolk	1 egg white, stiffly beaten

Cream the margarine until soft and then beat in the egg yolk. Gradually stir in the flour, salt and pepper to taste and the egg white. Shape into small balls, drop into boiling, salted water and simmer, with the lid on, for 5 minutes. Do not allow them to boil fast. When the dumplings are cooked, drain them and add to the hot soup.

Fried Flying Fish

Barbados has always been famous as the home of flying fish. However they are also found elsewhere in the Caribbean and today these delicacies are exported to other parts of the world.

This is an intricate fish to bone and fillet so I suggest you buy them ready-prepared.

juice of 2 medium limes	2 blades green shallots,
1 tbsp salt	sprig each of thyme and
1 cup water	marjoram, chopped
6 flying fish, filleted	very fine
1 small onion, chopped	1 egg, beaten lightly with
very fine	1 tbsp rum
salt and white pepper	breadcrumbs
dash of aromatic bitters	oil or lard for frying

Make a brine with the lime juice, salt and water, and soak the fish for 15 minutes. Rinse and dry. Mix the seasonings well and press firmly into spaces where bones have been removed. Dip each fish, both sides, into the egg then coat with breadcrumbs. Fry in hot oil/lard, filleted side down first, for 2-3 minutes each side.

Salt Fish Cakes

Salted cod fish – sometimes called bacalau – is known locally as salt fish. It used to be an important source of protein for many but more recently it has become expensive and is widely considered a delicacy. Of the several types available, 'box fish' is the least tedious to prepare.

8 oz/225 g salt fish	4 tbsp onion, finely chopped
6 medium potatoes, peeled	2 tbsp shallots, finely chopped
1 egg, beaten	1 tbsp parsley, finely chopped
½ tsp chilli, finely chopped	2 tbsp butter

Soak the fish in water overnight, then simmer in fresh water for about 20 minutes. Discard all bones and skin and flake very fine. Boil potatoes until tender and crush; mix with remaining ingredients. Shape into cakes and fry in hot fat until golden all over.

To serve as hors d'oeuvres, measure by teaspoon for dropping the mixture into the fat. These may be half cooked, drained, frozen and then heated quickly in hot fat or in the oven.

Okra Stew with Shrimp

This is a delectable spicy creole concoction and so easy to prepare. Great for a party! Be sure to purchase young, tender okras with no blemishes and to discard the tops when slicing.

1 lb/450 g medium shrimp, shelled and deveined
squeeze of lime juice
4 tbsp butter
2 medium sweet green peppers, deseeded and chopped
6 tbsp shallots/chives, chopped
8 oz/225 g/1 cup corn kernals, fresh, tinned or frozen

8 oz/225 g/1 cup okras, sliced
3 medium tomatoes, blanched, skinned and chopped
1 tbsp tomato paste
¼ tsp thyme
1 bay leaf
salt and pepper to taste
1 whole chilli pepper

Squeeze the lime juice over the shrimps. Heat butter in a frying pan and sauté the green pepper with shallots/chives for 2-3 minutes. Mix in remaining ingredients, except shrimp, and simmer for 10 minutes. Add the shrimps, return to boil and simmer for a further 5 minutes. Remove bay leaf and chilli before serving.